Comprehensive Guide on Methods, Tools, and Processes in Statistical Data Collection

Text book for college students

By:

Hilaria M. Barsabal, MA, MBA

Mariden V. Cauilan, DPA

By Hilaria M. Barsabal, Mariden V. Cauilan

ISBN:

Hardbound-978-621-470-813-0

Softbound/Paperback-978-621-470-814-7

PDF (downloadable)-978-621-470-815-4

Published by:

Poetry Planet Book Publishing House

Rosario, Pozorrubio, Pangasinan, Philippines

Contact Number: 09554960094

Email: maritesritumalta@gmail.com

Table of Content

Content **Page No.**

About this Book

A Comprehensive Guide on Methods, Tools, Processes, Variables, and Sources in Statistical Data Collection. The book covers the major steps involved in collecting data, including planning the data collection process, choosing appropriate data collection methods, designing data collection instruments, collecting data, and managing and storing data.

The book gives an in-depth look at the many data collection methods accessible, such as surveys, observational studies, experiments, and data mining approaches. It also looks at the benefits and drawbacks of each method, as well as how to choose the best method for a specific research subject.

Statistical Data Collection covers key concepts related to data collection, including sampling techniques, measurement scales, and data quality control. It also covers important considerations related to online data collection, such as security, ethics, and privacy.

The book includes real-world examples and practical tips for data collection, such as how to design effective surveys and how to collect and store data securely. It also provides guidance on how to analyze and interpret data collected using various methods.

A Comprehensive resource on Methods, Tools, Processes, Variables, and Sources in Statistical Data Collection is an essential resource for gathering and evaluating data for statistical analysis, whether you are a researcher, analyst, or student. This book will help you become a more skilled and confident data collection by providing clear and short explanations, practical suggestions, and extensive examples.

CHAPTER 1

Data Collection Fundamentals

Introduction:

In today's data-driven world, statistical data collection is a crucial aspect of research and decision-making. The accurate collection and analysis of data provides insights into trends, patterns, and relationships that can inform important decisions in various fields, from business and healthcare to politics and social sciences. Survey and interview instruments represent key tools for collecting data through direct interaction with individuals or groups. A comprehensive set of these instruments will help researchers and practitioners to build a strong foundation for their data analysis and decision-making. In this book, we will explore the importance of statistical data collection, the various types of survey and interview instruments, and the factors to consider when choosing the right tools for your research or project.

Definition

Statistical data collection is the process of gathering information or data from various sources using statistical methods. It involves the collection, analysis, and interpretation of data in a way that provides meaningful insights into a particular phenomenon or subject.

It is important because it helps in:

1. Making informed decisions: Statistical data collection helps in making informed decisions by providing accurate data that supports the decision-making process.

2. Identifying trends: By analyzing data over a period of time, trends can be identified and monitored, such as changes in consumer behavior, trading patterns or weather patterns.

3. Developing strategies: By analyzing statistical data it is possible to develop effective strategies to address issues or improve business processes.

4. Evaluating performance: Statistical data can be used to evaluate the performance of individuals, teams or organizations using metrics such as sales figures, customer satisfaction surveys or productivity statistics.

5. Identifying patterns: Statistical data can identify patterns and relationships that might not otherwise be noticed, such as associations between certain demographics and preferences or factors that are impacting production lines.

Overall, statistical data collection is an important tool in decision-making, monitoring performance, identifying patterns and developing effective strategies.

Data Collection

Data collection is the process of obtaining and collecting information from numerous sources in order to assess and make informed decisions based on the data acquired. This can include a variety of methods such as surveys, interviews, experiments, and observation.

It is critical to have a clear knowledge of what data is required and what the aim of the data collection is in order for data collection to be effective. Identifying the population or sample being investigated, establishing the variables to be assessed, and selecting appropriate procedures for data collection and recording are all examples of this.

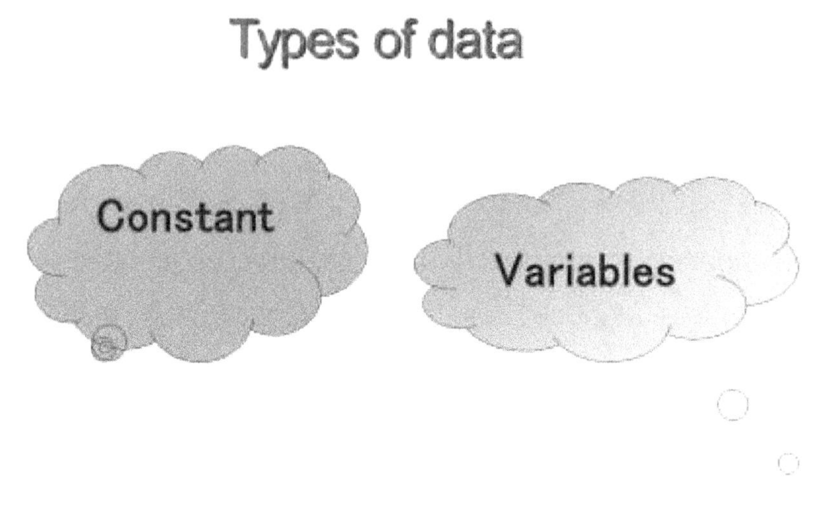

Definition of Constant and Variables

Constant: A constant is a fixed value that is utilized in expressions and equations. A constant is a fixed value that does not vary over time. For example, the size of a shoe, cloth, or other piece of clothing will not change at any moment.

Variable: Variables are phrases that can shift or change throughout time. In contrast to constants, its value does not remain constant. Variables include a person's height and weight, which do not always remain constant.

Difference Between Constants and Variables	
Constant	Variables

A constant's value does not vary over time.	A variable, on the other hand, changes its value depending on the formula being used.
Constants are frequently expressed numerically.	Variables are designated by letters or symbols..
Constants typically indicate known values in an equation, models, or line of programming.	Variables, on the other hand, indicate values that are uncertain.
The face values of constants are fixed.	Variables have no set face values.

Data is a particular measurement of a variable; it is the value you write in your data sheet. Data is typically classified into two types:

Classification of data:

- Quantitative
- Categorical or Qualitative

A variable with quantitative data is a variable using quantitative data; a variable with categorical data is a variable with categorical data. Each of these variables can be further subdivided.

Quantitative vs categorical variables

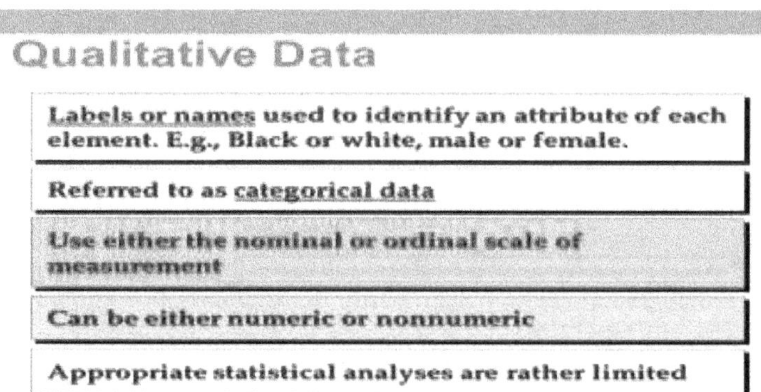

Quantitative Data

Quantitative data indicate how many or how much:

- Discrete, if measuring how many. E.g., number of 6-packs consumed at tail-gate party
- Continuous, if measuring how much. E.g., pounds of hamburger consumed at tail-gate party

Quantitative data are always numeric.

Ordinary arithmetic operations are meaningful for quantitative data.

Quantitative variables

When gathering quantitative data, the numbers that you enter represent real amounts that may be added, subtracted, divided, and so on. Quantitative variables are classified into two types: discrete and continuous.

Discrete vs continuous variables

Type of variable	What does the data represent?	Examples
Discrete variables (integer variables)	Individual item or value counts.	• Number of patients in a hospital • Number of different plant species in a botanical garden
Continuous variables (ratio variables)	Continuous or non-finite value measurements.	• weight • systolic blood pressure • Age

Categorical variables

Categorical variables represent several types of groupings. They are occasionally recorded as numbers, however the numbers signify categories rather than real quantities.

Categorical variables are classified into three types: binary, nominal, and ordinal variables.

Binary vs nominal vs ordinal variables

Type of variable	What does the data represent?	Examples
Binary variables (dichotomous variables)	The outcomes are	Win/lose in a contest Dead/Alive

	either yes or no.	True/ False
Nominal variables	There is no rank or order between these groups.	Labels, colors, plant species, gender
Ordinal variables	Groups that are arranged in a particular order.	In a survey, rating scale responses, such as Likert scales, year level of students, job positions.

Independent vs dependent variables

<u>Independent Variable</u>: The variable in the study under consideration. The cause for the outcome for the study.

<u>Dependent Variable</u>: The variable being affected by the independent variable. The effect of the study

$y = f(x)$

Which is which here?

Independent vs dependent vs control variables

Type of variable	**Definition**	**Example (experiment on salt tolerance)**
Independent variables (treatment variables)	Variables that you adjust to influence the outcome of an experiment.	The amount of salt provided to the water for every plant.
Dependent variables (response variables)	Variables that represent the experiment's outcome.	Any assessment of plant health and growth, such as plant height and wilting in this situation.
Control variables	Constant variables used throughout the investigation.	The temperature and lighting in the room where the plants are maintained, as well as the amount of water given to each plant.

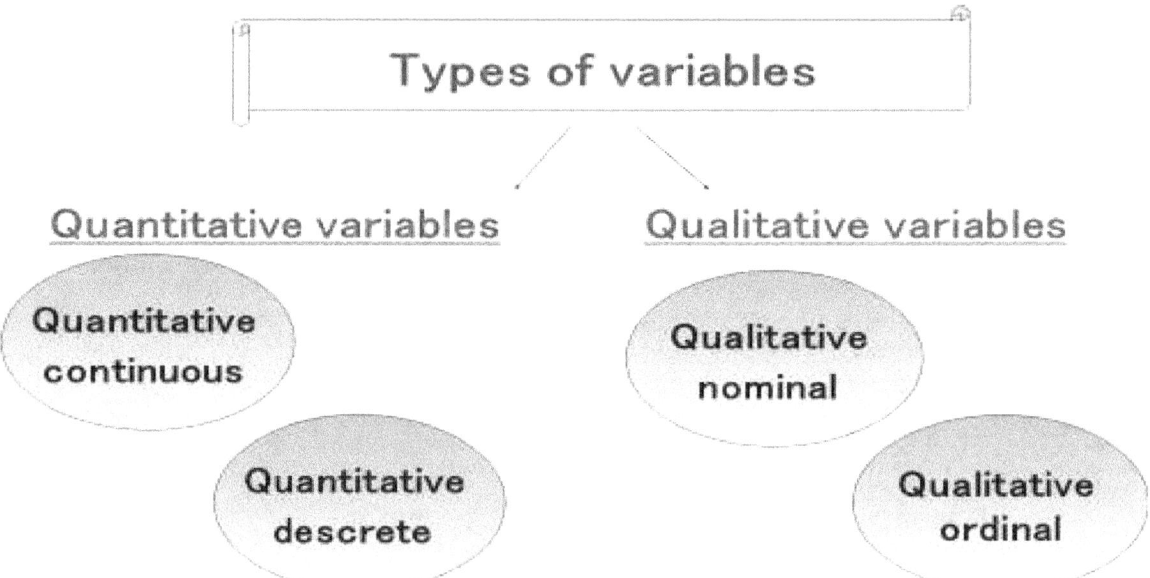

When it comes to data collection and analysis, quantitative research is concerned with numbers and figures, whereas qualitative research is concerned with words and meanings. Both are necessary for acquiring various types of knowledge.

Quantitative research is represented by numbers and graphs. It is used to test or corroborate theories and assumptions. This form of research can be utilized to develop generalizable truths about a subject.

Experiments, observations recorded as numbers, and surveys with closed-ended questions are examples of common quantitative procedures.

Information bias, omitted variable bias, sample bias, and selection bias are all risks in quantitative research.

Other common types of variables

You will be able to choose the appropriate statistical test once you have identified your independent and dependent variables and determined whether they are categorical or quantitative.

However, there are numerous additional ways to describe variables that will aid in the interpretation of your data. Some useful variables are provided here.

Type of variable	Definition	Example (experiment on salt tolerance)
Confounding variables	A variable in your experiment that conceals the true influence of another variable. This can occur when another variable is strongly related to a variable of interest but is not controlled in your experiment. Confounding factors have a high danger of bringing a range of research biases into your work, including omitted variable bias.	Plant survival may be affected by pot size and soil type just as much as by salt inputs. These potential confounders would be controlled in an experiment by holding them constant.
Latent variables	A variable that cannot be directly measured but can be represented via a substitute.	Plant salt tolerance cannot be tested directly, but it can be extrapolated from plant health metrics in our salt-addition trial.
Variables that are composites	A variable created in an experiment by merging various variables. These variables are formed when data is analyzed rather than measured.	To make it easier to communicate your findings, you may combine the three plant health variables into a single plant-health score.

In statistics, variables or numbers are defined and classified using various measuring scales. Each level of measurement scale has unique qualities that influence the diverse applications of statistical analysis. In this post, we will learn about four different types of scales: nominal, ordinal, interval, and ratio scales.

What exactly is the scale?

A scale is a device or thing that may be utilized to measure or quantify any event or object.

Levels of Measurements

There are four different measurement scales. The data can be classified as one of four scales. The four sorts of scales are as follows:

- **Nominal Scale**
- **Ordinal Scale**
- **Interval Scale**
- **Ratio Scale**

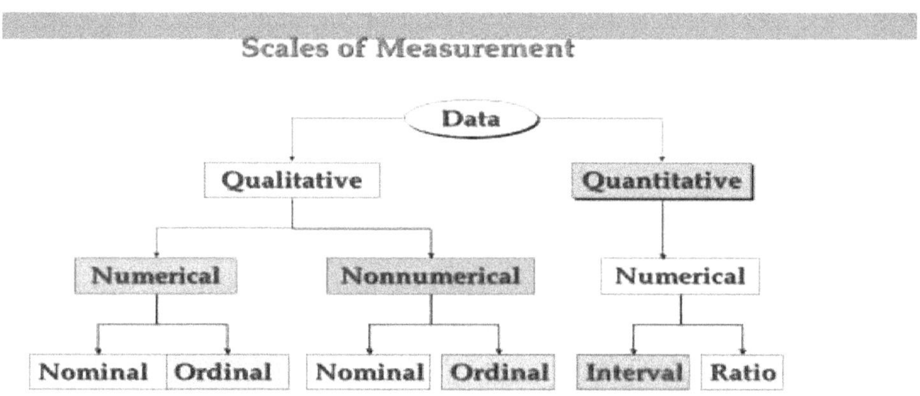

Nominal Scale:

A nominal scale is the first level of measuring scale in which the numbers act as "tags" or "labels" to classify or identify the items. A nominal scale typically deals with non-numeric variables or numbers that have no meaning.

Characteristics of Nominal Scale

- ✓ A nominal scale variable is divided into two or more groups. The response should fall into one of the classifications in this measurement mechanism.
- ✓ It is of high quality. The numbers are used to identify the objects in this case.
- ✓ The numbers do not define the qualities of the thing. In the nominal scale, the only allowed element of numbers is "counting."

Scales of Measurement

- **Nominal**

Example:
Students of a university are classified by the cources they enrolled. BSLMS, BSRT, BSPH, BSEd and so on.

A numeric code can be used for the school variable (e.g. 1: BSLMS, 2: BSRT 3: BSPH, and so on).

Ordinal Scale

The ordinal scale is the second level of measurement, reporting data ordering and ranking without identifying the degree of variance between them. Ordinal data is also known as qualitative data or categorical data since it represents "order." It can be categorized, named, and ranked.

Characteristics of the Ordinal Scale

- ✓ The ordinal scale displays the variables' relative ranking.
- ✓ It detects and describes a variable's magnitude.
- ✓ Ordinal scales provide ranks of variables in addition to the information provided by the nominal scale.
- ✓ The qualities of the intervals remain unknown.
- ✓ Surveyors can immediately assess the level of agreement on the identified sequence of variables

Scales of Measurement

Ordinal

Example:

Students of a university are classified by their class standing using a nonnumeric label such as Freshman, Sophomore, Junior, or Senior.

A numeric code can be used for the class standing variable (e.g. 1 denotes Freshman, 2 denotes Sophomore, and so on).

Interval Scale

The interval scale is the third measuring level. It is described as a quantitative measurement scale with a meaningful difference between two variables. In other words, the variables are measured precisely rather than relatively, where the presence of zero is arbitrary.

Characteristics of Interval Scale:

- ✓ The interval scale is quantitative in the sense that it can quantify the difference between values.
- ✓ It is possible to compute the mean and median of the variables.
- ✓ You can understand the difference between the variables by subtracting their values.
- ✓ The interval scale is the preferred scale in statistics because it allows any numerical value to be assigned to arbitrary assessments such as moods, calendar types, and so on.

Scales of Measurement

Example: Average Starting Salary Offer for the year 2021
For Nurses, Medical Technologies, Pharmacist
And other health care professionals

Ratio Scale

The ratio scale is the quantitative fourth level of measurement scale. It is a changeable measurement scale. It enables scientists to compare differences or intervals. The ratio scale has a distinguishing feature. It has the appearance of the origin or zero points.

Characteristics of Ratio Scale:

- ✓ The absolute zero feature of the ratio scale
- ✓ Because of the zero-point characteristic, it does not contain negative numbers.
- ✓ It provides unique chances for statistical analysis. The variables can be orderly added, subtracted, multiplied, and divided. The ratio scale can be used to compute the mean, median, and mode.
- ✓ The ratio scale offers unique and beneficial qualities. One such feature is that it permits unit conversions such as kilogram - calories, gram - calories, and so on.

Scales of Measurement

Example:
The salaries of Policemen is 2.5 times higher than the salaries of medical technologies in the Philippines

Scale by which the variables are measured

NOMINAL
- Always qualitative
- Categories are simply labels and cannot be used nor meaningful for ranking
- Examples: colors (red, white, blue); regions (Luzon, Visayas, Mindanao)

ORDINAL
- Can be qualitative or quantitative
- Categories have an inherent or implied ranking system
- Quantitative categories simply measure the order or rank rather than the actual value
- Example: SES status (low, medium, high); severity of disease (mild; moderate severe); ranking of students according to academic achievement (1, 2, 3, etc.)

INTERVAL
- Always quantitative
- Exact differences between categories can be measured but the zero point is arbitrary
- Example: temperature (measured in centigrade or Fahrenheit); grades (1.0, 1.25, 1.5, 1.75, etc)

RATIO
- Always quantitative
- Has a fixed zero point
- The ratio of one number over another can be computed and meaningfully interpreted
- Most quantitative variable are in the ratio scale of measurement
- Examples: age; height; weight; serum cholesterol levels, etc.

The Hierarchy of Levels

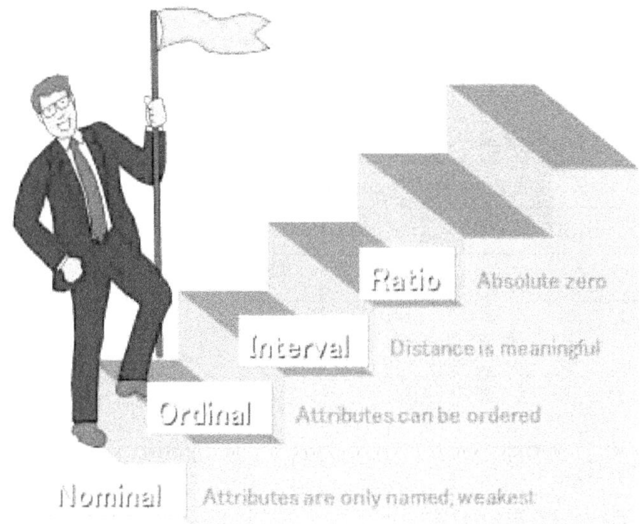

Exercise 1

A. Determine what variable type given the following:	Variable type
1. Systolic Blood pressure	
2. Body Mass Index	

3. Size of a container	
4. Men's waist line	
5. Number of enrollees	
6. Number of Patients confined in a hospital	
7. Car speed	
8. Customer satisfaction	
9. Identification Number	
10. Diastolic blood pressure	

B. Determine which variables are qualitative and which are quantitative.	**Classification of variables**
11. Systolic Blood pressure	
12. Body Mass Index	
13. Size of a container	
14. Men's waist line	
15. Number of enrollees	
16. Number of Patients confined in a hospital	
17. Car speed	
18. Customer satisfaction	
19. Identification Number	
20. Diastolic blood pressure	

Determine which variables are discrete and which are continuous.	
1. Number of COVID patients in the region	
2. Plant species in a botanical garden	
3. Height of Patients in meters	
4. Weight of children in pounds	

5. Number of HIV patients	
6. Monthly Salary of employees	
7. Number of bottle containers in the laboratory room	
8. Number of employees infected with COVID 19 virus	
9. Different types of COVID 19 virus in the country	
10. Systolic Blood pressure	

CHAPTER 2

Data Collection Methods

Introduction

The procedure of gathering data is critical to the success of any research effort. Choosing between primary and secondary data, as well as qualitative or quantitative methodologies, might have an impact on the study's results. In this chapter, we'll look at different sorts of data gathering methods and how they can be used to gain useful insights and information. This chapter provides a full overview of the data collection process, from exploring the benefits and drawbacks of primary and secondary data to digging into the complexities of qualitative and quantitative data. So, let's get started and investigate the complexities of data collection for research purposes.

Types of Data Collection

PRIMARY DATA

The technique of acquiring unique and personal information directly from the source or target population is known as primary data collection. This sort of data collection entails gathering information that has not previously been obtained, recorded, or publicized. Surveys, interviews, observations, experiments, and focus groups are all approaches for gathering primary data. The data gathered is usually particular to the research question or purpose and can provide useful insights that secondary data sources cannot provide. In market research, social research, and scientific research, primary data collection is frequently used.

Secondary Data

Secondary data collection is the process of acquiring information from previously acquired and evaluated sources rather than performing new research to collect primary data. Secondary data sources include published reports, books, journals, newspapers, websites, government publications, and other materials.

Qualitative Data

Qualitative data gathering techniques such as interviews, focus groups, observations, and document analysis are used to acquire non-numerical data such as opinions, experiences, perceptions, and feelings. It is frequently employed in the social sciences, psychology, and humanities to grasp the deeper meaning and context of a phenomena or situation. Qualitative data collection approaches provide for a more in-depth and comprehensive study of research questions, as well as rich and nuanced insights into human behavior and experiences.

Qualitative Data Collection

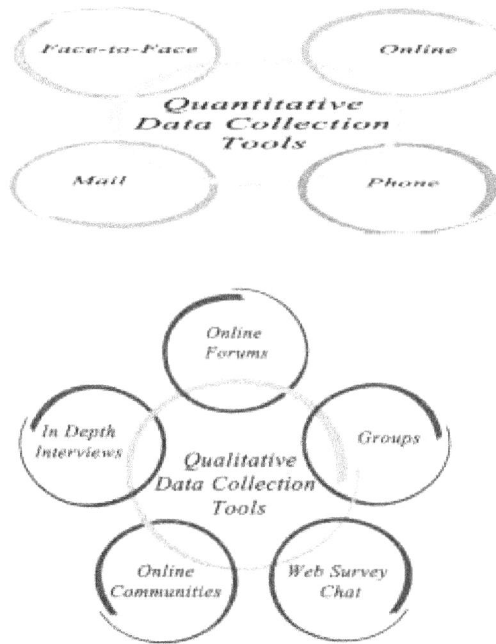

Quantitative Data

Quantitative data collection is a technique for gathering numerical data that may be examined statistically. Surveys, experiments, and other structured data gathering approaches are commonly used to collect this information. Quantitative data collection aims to quantitatively and objectively quantify and measure variables such as actions, attitudes, and views. This information is frequently used to test hypotheses, identify trends, and create relationships among variables. Methods for collecting quantitative data allow for precise measurement and generalization of findings to a larger population. It is frequently used in economics, psychology, and natural sciences.

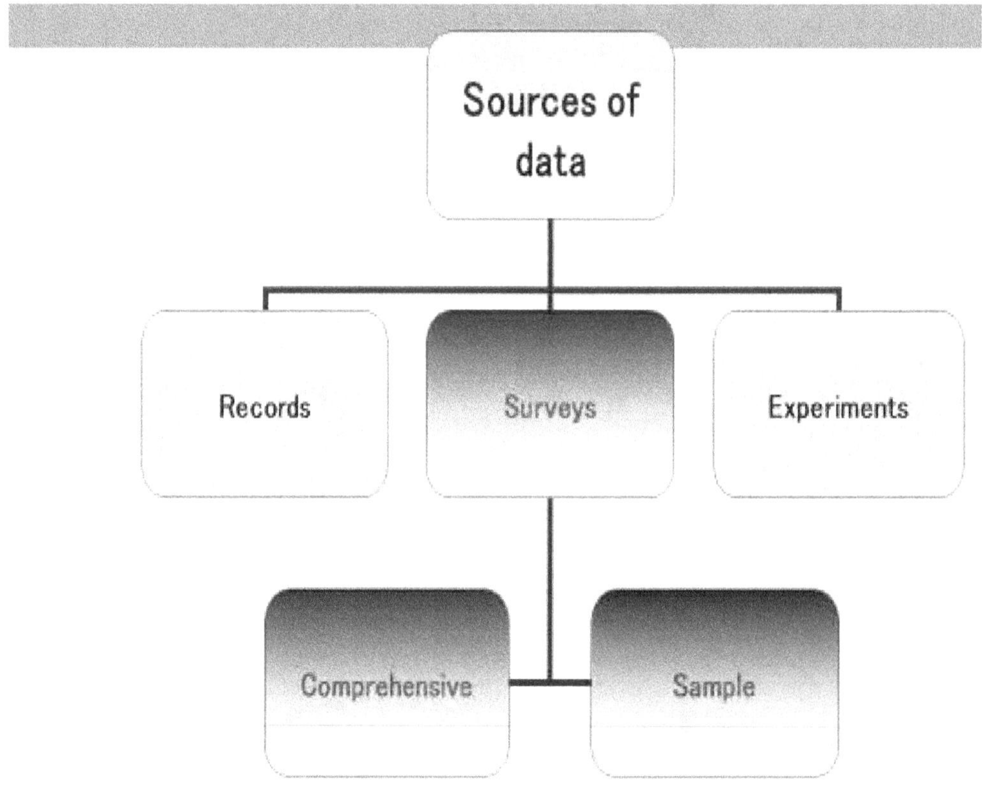

DATA COLLECTION METHODS

- ***Survey***
- ***Interview***
- ***Focus groups***
- ***Observation***
- ***Experiment***
- **Secondary data analysis**

Surveys involve asking questions to a sample of individuals or organizations to collect data. Surveys can be conducted in person, over the phone, or online.

A **survey** is a type of research approach in which data is collected and analyzed from a group of people. A **questionnaire** is a specific tool or instrument for data collection.

Creating valid and trustworthy questions that fulfill your research objectives, arranging them in a useful order, and selecting an effective method of administration are all part of the questionnaire design process.

However, creating a questionnaire is only one aspect of survey research. Defining the population of interest, selecting an appropriate sampling strategy, administering questionnaires, data cleansing and analysis, and interpretation are all part of survey research.

Sampling is vital in survey research since you will frequently want to generalize your findings to the entire population. For externally valid results, collect data from a sample that represents the spectrum of opinions in the population. There will always be some disparities between the population and the sample, but limiting these differences will help you avoid numerous types of research bias, such as sampling bias, ascertainment bias, and under coverage bias.

Questionnaire Techniques

- ➢ Questionnaires that are self-administered
- ➢ Questionnaires distributed by researchers

Self-administered questionnaires can be delivered online, in person, or via mail. All questions are standardized, ensuring that all respondents receive the same questions with the same wording.

Advantages of Questionnaires that are self-administered can be:

- ✓ Economical
- ✓ Simple to administer for both small and big groups
- ✓ Confidential and appropriate for delicate issues
- ✓ Individualized

They could, however, also be:

- People with inadequate reading or verbal capabilities nonresponse bias (the majority of those invited may not complete the questionnaire)
- People who volunteer are favored since impersonal survey requests are frequently ignored.

Questionnaires distributed by researchers

Researcher-administered questionnaires are phone, in-person, or online interviews between researchers and respondents.

Questionnaires distributed by researchers can:

- ✓ Assist you in ensuring that the respondents are representative of your target audience
- ✓ Allow for clarification of problematic or unclear questions and answers
- ✓ Have high response rates because it is more difficult to deny an interview when respondents receive personal attention

  However, questionnaires administered by researchers can be resource-constrained. They are as follows:

  - Expensive and time-consuming to carry out
  - If you have qualitative responses, it will be more difficult to analyze.
  - Prone to experimenter bias or demand characteristics because of the lack of anonymity, replies are more likely to exhibit social desirability bias.

Open-ended vs. closed-ended questions

Your questionnaire might include open-ended or closed-ended questions, or a combination of the two.

Using **closed-ended questions** restricts your responses, whereas **open-ended questions** allow for a wide range of responses. You must balance these issues with your available time and resources.

Closed-ended questions

Closed-ended, or restricted-choice, questions present respondents with a limited selection of options from which to choose. Closed-ended inquiries are ideal for gathering information on categorical or quantitative factors.

Categorical variables might be nominal or ordinal. Quantitative variables could represent an interval or ratio. Understanding the type of variable and the amount of measurement allows you to do proper statistical studies for generalizable outcomes.

Closed-ended question examples for various variables

Nominal variables include non-rankable characteristics such as race or ethnicity. This contains categories that are binary or dichotomous.

It is ideal to have categories that are mutually exclusive and include all conceivable answers. There should be no overlap in the responses.

In binary or dichotomous questions, respondents will have only two options to pick from.

Example: Nominal variables

What is your primary occupation?
( ) Farmer
( ) Teacher
( ) Office Worker
( ) Engineer
( ) Military uniformed Personnel
( ) Lawyer
( ) Others please specify___________

Are you happy with your present work-from-home policies?
( ) Yes
( ) No

Example: Ordinal variables

What is your current year level?
( ) First
( ) Second
( ) Third

( ) Fourth
( ) Fifth

What is your present age in years?
( ) 18 or below
( ) 19
( ) 20
( ) 21
( ) 22 or above

Likert scale inquiries use rating scales to capture ordinal data.
Example: Likert-type questions

How satisfied or dissatisfied are you with your online delivery mode of instruction this semester?

( ) Very dissatisfied
( ) Some-what dissatisfied
( ) Neither satisfied nor dissatisfied
( ) Somewhat satisfied
( ) Very satisfied

When there are four or more Likert-type questions, the composite data can be treated as quantitative data on an interval scale. Multiple Likert-type questions are used in intelligence tests, psychological scales, and personality surveys to collect interval data.

Strong statistical hypothesis testing can be used with interval or ratio scales to suit your research objectives.

The advantages and disadvantages of closed-ended questions

Closed-ended questions that are well-designed are simple to grasp and respond to swiftly. However, you may still overlook important responses that are valuable to responders. Due to an inadequate set of response items, some respondents may be forced to select the closest alternative to their genuine answer. These types of queries may potentially leave out important information.

Open-ended questions

Open-ended questions, also known as long-form inquiries, allow respondents to react in their own terms. Respondents can respond in ways that researchers may not have considered otherwise because there are no constraints on their options. For example, instead of selecting from a limited list, respondents may prefer to answer "multiracial" for the race question.

To address these issues, provide somewhat closed-ended questions with an open-ended option for respondents to fill in their individual answers.

Interviews are conducted one-on-one between the interviewer and the respondent. Structured or unstructured interviews can be done in person or over the phone.

An interview is a face-to-face talk between two people conducted solely for the aim of gathering information for a research project. Each of the three basic forms of interviews, planned, semi-structured, and unstructured, differs differently from the others. Interviews can be conducted in a group or one-on-one setting. Data can be documented during interviews using stenography, videotaping, audiotaping, or written notes.

Structured interviews are basically questionnaires that are administered verbally. It is shallow in depth and usually just takes a few minutes to finish. It is renowned for its speed and effectiveness, but it lacks depth.

Unstructured Interviews - An in-depth interview that allows the researcher to collect a wide range of information for a specified goal.

Even though it takes more effort, this technique allows a researcher to combine structure and flexibility.

Advantages

- ✓ Information in detail
- ✓ The ability to be adaptable
- ✓ Precise information

Disadvantages

- Time-consuming
- Expensive to collect.

Semi-structured Interviews In this method, there are a number of critical questions that address the breadth of study fields. It gives the researcher more freedom to dive further into the issue. In this technique, there are a few key questions that cut across the span of research topics. It enables the researcher to explore further into the topic.

Focus groups This data collection technique emphasizes qualitative research, which is the polar opposite of quantitative research, which uses numerical data. It is within the major category of information based on the respondents' thoughts and feelings. A group of volunteers, usually between 6 and 10, will be asked open-ended questions to provide input for this study.

Advantages

- ✓ The information received is usually very detailed.
- ✓ It delivers outcomes in a timely and efficient manner.
- ✓ It is less expensive as compared to one-on-one interviews.

Disadvantages

- Inadequate going into sufficient detail to address a topic's finer points.
- Bias may still be present.
- Interviewer training is required.

- The outcome is mostly outside the researcher's control.
- A few loud yells can drown out the others.
- Difficulty in assembling a diverse group.

Observation: The process of monitoring or viewing a subject while acquiring data is known as observation. An active source of information must be actively obtained during observation. Using scientific instruments, data can also be perceived and captured during an observation. Observations are sometimes conducted continuously or over time. Structured, unstructured, and semi-structured observations are just a handful of the many possible varieties. It is the process of observing and recording the behavior of people, objects, or events in their natural environment. Depending on the study question, observation might be done overtly or covertly.

Case studies are in-depth examinations of a single person, organization, or event. Case studies are used to learn more about a certain occurrence. A case study is a detailed account of a technique, system, or event at a single company. Case studies employ survey, use data, and qualitative data collection approaches. Prior to conducting qualitative research, quantitative data must be gathered.

Experiments involve fiddling with one or more variables and seeing the effect on another variable. Experiments are commonly used in scientific research. Experiments are used to investigate causal relationships. You alter one or more independent variables and assess their impact on one or more dependent variables.

Secondary data analysis is the utilization of previously collected data for a different purpose. Secondary data can be obtained from a variety of sources, including government agencies, academic institutions, and private companies. It requires validating existing information in databases, reports, meeting minutes, financial records, newsletters, and so on. It is a cost-effective way of data collecting. However, it is not always the entire data source.

Exercises 2

A. Identify which statistical scale of measurement applies for the following variables.

_________________1. Patients in the hospital

_________________2.Light intensity

_________________3. Room Temperature

_________________4.Environmental awareness

_________________5.Emotional intelligence

_________________6.Number of accidents

_________________7.Vehicle speed

_________________8.Allowance of students

_________________9. Type of School Enrolled

_________________10. Doctors' preference

B. Specify which of the following variables are qualitative or quantitative.

_________________1. Hospitals bed capacity

_________________2. Number of patients infected with CVID 19 in the Philippines

_________________3. Prescription of a doctor to his patients

_________________4. Collected type of blood samples

_________________5.Blood type

_________________6. Doctors' Fee

_________________7.Vehicle speed

_________________8.Allowance of students per day

________________9. School Fees

________________10. Blood pressure of a patient

C. Specify which of the following quantitative variables are discrete or continues

________________1. Hospitals bed capacity

________________2. Number of patients infected with CVID 19 in the Philippines

________________3. Cagayan State University Campuses

________________4. Collected type of blood samples

________________5.Diastolic Blood Pressure

________________6. Doctors' Fee

________________7.Vehicle speed

________________8.Allowance of students per day

________________9. Number of Nurses employed at the Cagayan Valley Medical Center

________________10. Body Temperature

CHAPTER 3

DATA COLLECTION PROCESS

Introduction:

Data collection is an integral part of any research project. It involves gathering information on a specific topic through various methods such as surveys, interviews, observations, and document analysis. The process of data collection requires careful planning and execution to ensure that the information gathered is accurate, reliable, and relevant to the research question. In this chapter, we will explore the different methods of data collection, their strengths and limitations, and the factors that influence the choice of methods. We will also examine the various tools and techniques used to collect and analyze data, and the ethical considerations involved in data collection. By gaining a deeper understanding of the data collection process, researchers can generate high-quality data and make informed decisions to enhance the validity and reliability of their findings.

How to Collect Data?

The following are some steps to consider when collecting data:

Step 1. Determine the objective: Before you begin collecting data, you must identify the study's objective. This will assist you in determining what data you will need to collect and how you will acquire it.

Step 2. Identify the data sources: Establish the data sources that will assist you in achieving your goal. These sources can be either primary (surveys, interviews, and observations) or secondary (books, journals, and databases).

Step 3. Determine the data collecting method: Once you've identified the data sources, you'll need to figure out how to gather the data. This could be accomplished by online surveys, phone interviews, or in-person meetings.

Step 4. Create a data collecting plan: Create a plan outlining the steps you'll take to collect the data. The timeline, tools and equipment required, and persons involved should all be included in this strategy.

Step 5. Test the data collection process: Before you begin collecting data, confirm that the data collection procedure is effective and efficient.

Step 6. Collect the data: Gather the data in accordance with the plan you devised in step 4.

Step 1 Determining the objectives:

One of the most significant tasks in objective formulation is to convert abstract concepts offered in a theoretical or conceptual framework into observable, quantifiable, and operational indicators.

Suppose a study on factors affecting the level of the academic performance has the conceptual framework shown in Figure 1.

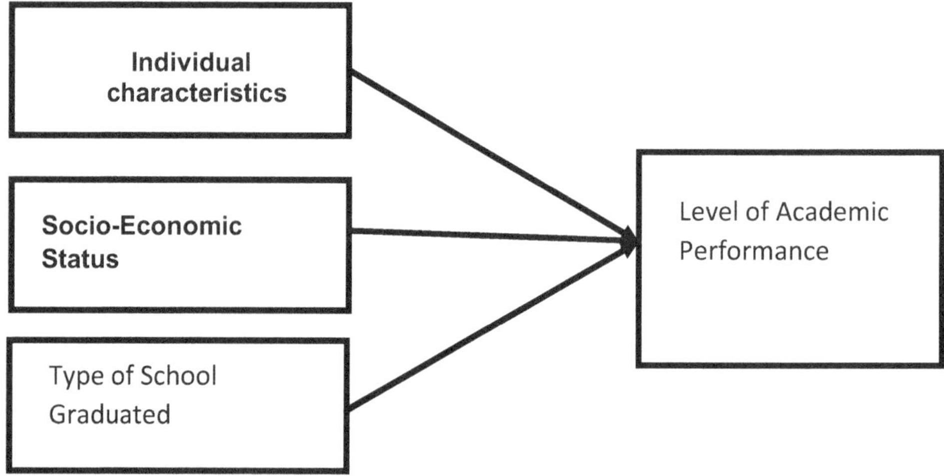

Figure 1. Factors Affecting the Level of Academic Performance of an Individual

To make the research more feasible, the researcher might opt to just focus on the effect of individual characteristics in his study. However, the phrase "individual characteristics" is still an abstraction because there are so many kinds of individual characteristics. In addition, there is still also a need to convert the variable "level of academic performance of an individual" into measurable and operational terms, because there are so many ways to measure this concept. Therefore, one way of formulating the general and specific objectives based on the conceptual framework presented in Figure 1 is as follows:

General objective:

To determine if there is a relationship between the characteristics of an individual and his/her level of academic performance.

Specific objective:

To determine if there is a relationship between a student's economic status and his/her level of performance.

Step 2 Identify the Data Source

The data you acquire may be primary or secondary data, and it may be gathered by organizations through experiments or surveys, or by individual workers. As you can see, there are various sources of data in statistics.

In statistics, you must collect data and facts that can be numerically measured. Simply put, data is a collection of similar observations.

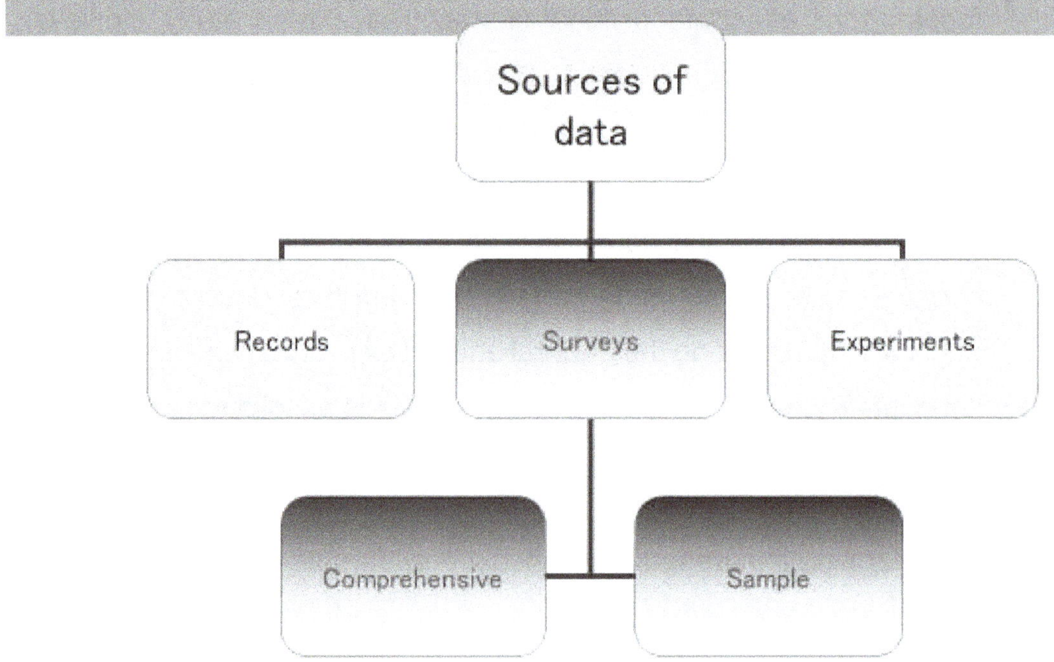

There are two categories of data sources: statistical and non-statistical. Statistical sources are data that is collected for official purposes, such as censuses and officially run surveys. Non-statistical sources are data collected for other administrative or private sector goals.

The following are the two sources of data:

Sources within the organization

Internal sources are when data is gathered from reports and records kept by the organization itself.

For example, a corporation may issue an annual report detailing its profit and loss, total sales, loans, wages, and so on.

Outside sources

External sources are data sources that are gathered from outside the organization. For example, if a tour and travel company acquires tourism statistics from the Karnataka Transport Corporation, this is referred to as an external source of data.

Step 3 Determining the data collection method

Primary data is information gathered personally by a researcher or a group of researchers for a specific research endeavor or objective. It is new information that has not previously been published or analyzed, and it is obtained directly from the source or through data gathering methods such as surveys, interviews, observations, and experiments.

Primary Data Collection Methods

- Surveys are one of the most prevalent types of primary data collection procedures. They entail posing a series of standardized questions to a sample of individuals or organizations, typically via a questionnaire or an online form.
- Oral investigation, indirect - Interviews entail asking a sample of persons or groups open-ended or organized questions in person, over the phone, or via video conferencing. They can be conducted one-on-one or in a focus group environment.
- Observations are the systematic recording of people' or groups' behavior or activities in a natural or controlled situation. This method of data collecting is commonly employed in anthropology, sociology, and psychology.
- Experiments entail varying one or more factors and observing the effects on a desired outcome. In scientific study, they are frequently employed to establish cause-and-effect correlations.
- Case studies entail an in-depth examination of a specific individual, group, or organization. They usually entail gathering a variety of data, such as interviews, observations, and documents.

Step 4. Creating data collection plan

A data collection strategy is a method for gathering precise information about your target audience. You may use it to learn more about what people like and dislike, what inspires them, how they react to various messages, and how they use the content you provide. A effective data collecting strategy will also enable you to forecast future patterns in your target population.

A **data collection** plan is a document that details how you intend to collect information from your users and clients. It's a step-by-step method on gathering and storing client information.

It's also a good approach to ensure that all of the steps in your process are properly documented and structured. A data collection strategy also serves as a means of communicating with your team and stakeholders about the information you're attempting to collect, why you need it, when you need it, how you'll obtain it, and who will get it.

A data collection plan is a document that details how you intend to collect information from your users and clients. It's a step-by-step method on gathering and storing client information.

It's also a good approach to ensure that all of the steps in your process are properly documented and structured. A data collection strategy also serves as a means of communicating with your team and stakeholders about the information you're attempting to collect, why you need it, when you need it, how you'll obtain it, and who will get it.

Why Do You Need a Data Collection Plan?

Data collection plans are an excellent technique to guarantee that your research is as precise and comprehensive as feasible.

A data collection plan is intended to assist you in collecting data from your subjects and reporting their results. It can be used to establish how much data is required, how it will be measured, where the data will be gathered and supplied, who will collect it all, whether a sample or the entire population will be measured, and how the information will be presented.

Data collecting plans can also assist you in determining if an internet survey or a paper questionnaire is required. A data gathering strategy can be used for a variety of purposes, including:

1. Making decisions regarding which metrics to track (for example, number of transactions vs. number of users)
2. Setting objectives for gathering information about your client or customer base (for example, the number of new consumers each quarter)
3. Data collection can be time-consuming and expensive. Without a data gathering strategy, you risk missing out on key insights that might help your organization flourish.
4. Having all of this information in one place allows everyone on your team to remain on top of things—and allows you to make changes as needed.

How Should a Data Collection Strategy Be Used?

The most effective approach to accomplish this is through data gathering plans. They can be used to improve your understanding of your audience, highlight areas for improvement or expansion, and forecast future patterns.

Using a data collecting plan also allows you to customize the material you create for your audience, which keeps them engaged and interested in your business. This can help your company grow faster than before.

How to Make a Data Collection Plan?

1. Determine the questions you want to answer. What are your objectives for this project? Is there anything in particular about your organization or your customers' behavior or wants that you'd like to learn more about? What kind of data might be useful in answering such questions? Do any other stakeholders have any queries they'd like answered?
2. Determine the type of data that is available. Is any private information shared with third parties, such as vendors or contractors; if so, can you provide them access to portion of this information without jeopardizing your competitive advantage? If not, what forms of open-source information (such as blog postings or social media posts) are available to give insight into your clients' views and sentiments about your services and products?
3. Determine the amount of data required; this may necessitate extra questions before proceeding to measure your data.
4. Determine where the data will be collected. Whether it's through an online survey, a phone call, or another method entirely.
5. Choose whether to measure a subset of the population or the entire population. Some studies require only one person's opinion, while others may require the opinions of 500 people. And some studies only collect data on one type of individual (such as gender), whilst others may collect data on several other sorts of persons at the same time (such as age and income).
6. Determine the format in which the data will be displayed. Do you want all of it in text or all of it in charts?

Step 5. Test the data collection process:

Once you've decided on a data collection technique and plan, make sure your measuring methods are accurate and that you're gathering the information you need. Accurate measures are essential for data gathering because the data you collect can assist you in making decisions, and having accurate data measurements, particularly for quantitative data, can assist you in making the best judgments for your business. This stage is especially significant since it can help you determine the best data gathering methods for your specific needs and help you design rigorous data collection strategies.

Step 6. Collect the data:

After developing plans and techniques for gathering the desired data, you can put those plans into action. This can be the most time-consuming step in the data gathering process because you may wish to collect hundreds of data points depending on the type of information you want and the method you utilize. Because some approaches, such as social media monitoring, are ongoing, establishing a start and end date for data gathering might assist you in processing the information more correctly. Others, such as interviews and research, can be done quickly but require more time to understand.

Exercise 3

1. Explain the difference between Primary and Secondary Data.	2. Briefly discuss the data gathering process
3. Discuss the importance of creating data collection plan.	**4. What are the different factors to be considered in creating data collection plan?**

5. Explain how data collection strategy be used?	**6. Discuss the different sources of data.**

CHAPTER 4

Application of Data Collection

Introduction

In today's data-driven world, businesses, organizations, and individuals are constantly looking for insights and answers from data. Data collection is critical for informing decisions, finding trends and patterns, and ultimately driving progress. Data collecting has numerous applications in healthcare, finance, education, and other fields.

Technological advancements have permitted the collecting of massive amounts of data from diverse sources. However, without effective data collecting and management systems in place, the sheer volume of data can be daunting. Furthermore, how data is used might be the difference between a company's or organization's success or failure.

This chapter will dive into the various applications of data collection, including the different data types, methods, and technologies used. We will explore how data collection is used in various fields and industries, highlighting its importance and impact. Additionally, we will examine some of the challenges related to data collection and management, as well as provide insights on best practices for effective data collection.

Methods of data gathering are widely utilized in a variety of disciplines, including social sciences, healthcare, business, education, and others. Here are some examples of data collection methods used in various fields:

Healthcare: gathering methods are used in healthcare to assess patient health and track treatment outcomes. Electronic health records and medical charts are routinely used to collect data on patients' medical histories, diagnoses, and treatments. Researchers may also employ clinical trials and surveys to acquire data on the efficacy of various treatments.

Education: Data gathering methods are used in education to assess student performance and measure the effectiveness of teaching approaches. Standardized tests, quizzes, and exams are frequently used to collect data on student learning results. Teachers may also collect statistics on teaching efficacy through classroom observation and student feedback.

Social scientists frequently collect data from individuals or groups using surveys, questionnaires, and interviews. They may also collect data on social behaviors and interactions through observation. This information is frequently utilized to research human behavior, attitudes, and beliefs.

Business: Data collection methods are used by businesses to obtain information on consumer behavior, market trends, and rival activity. Customer surveys, sales reports, and market research studies may be used to collect data. This information is used to help businesses make decisions, create marketing strategies, and improve products and services.

Agriculture: Farmers collect data to monitor crop growth and health. Data on soil moisture, temperature, and nutrient levels can be collected using sensors and remote sensing technology. This information is utilized to maximize agricultural yields and reduce waste.

Environmental scientists collect data in order to monitor air and water quality, follow climatic patterns, and assess the influence of human activity on the environment. They may collect data on environmental conditions using sensors, satellite images, and laboratory analysis.

Transportation businesses collect data in order to track vehicle performance, optimize routes, and improve safety. Data on vehicle speed, fuel usage, and driver behavior is collected via GPS systems, on-board sensors, and other tracking technologies.

Purpose of Data Collection

The goal of collecting data varies based on the setting and goals of the study, but in general, it serves to:

Provide information: Data gathering provides information about a certain phenomenon or behavior that may be utilized to better understand it.

Support decision-making: Data gathering provides decision-makers with evidence-based information that can be utilized to inform policies, plans, and actions.

Measure progress: Data collecting can be used to assess the effectiveness of initiatives or programs meant to address a specific issue or problem.

Identify trends: collecting data can aid in the identification of trends and patterns that may suggest changes in behaviors or outcomes over time.

Data gathering can be used to **track and analyze** the implementation and impact of policies, programs, and initiatives.

When to use Data Collection

Data collection is utilized when it is necessary to obtain information or data on a specific topic or phenomenon. It is commonly used in research, assessment, and monitoring, and it is critical for making informed decisions and improving outcomes.

Gathering data is very beneficial in the following scenarios:

- **Research**: Data collection is used in research to acquire information on variables of interest in order to answer research questions and test hypotheses.
- **Decision-making:** Data collecting is used to provide information to decision-makers that can be utilized to inform policies, plans, and actions.
- **Quality improvement**: Data collection is used in quality improvement activities to identify areas for improvement and to track progress toward goals
- **Monitoring**: Data gathering is used in monitoring to assess progress toward goals or targets, as well as to identify any areas that need to be addressed.
- **Evaluation**: In the evaluation of a program, data collection is used to analyze the success of programs or interventions and to find areas for improvement.

Exercise 4

1. Briefly discuss the purpose of data collection.	2. Explain how data collection be utilized in different fields.

3. **Discuss how data collection be utilized in decision making process.**	4. **Give examples how data collection be used in quality improvement.**

5. **What are some scenarios where data collection is essential in evaluation?**	6. **In what instance were data collection is necessary in monitoring?**

CHAPTER 5

The use Likert Scale of Measurement

Introduction:

In research, collecting data is a critical step towards achieving the desired outcome. Accurate and reliable data collection enables researchers to draw meaningful conclusions and make informed decisions. One of the most commonly used scales for measuring attitudes, perceptions, and beliefs in research is the Likert scale. This scale is widely used because it is easy to understand, administer, and interpret. The scale compiles a range of responses on a set of statements from strongly disagree to strongly agree. This chapter introduces readers to the use of the Likert scale in data collection in research. It discusses the advantages and limitations of the scale, as well as the steps involved in designing a Likert scale questionnaire. The chapter also explores the analysis and interpretation of Likert scale data, including the use of descriptive statistics and statistical inference techniques. With a thorough understanding of the Likert scale, researchers can design questionnaires that provide reliable data, leading to accurate and valid conclusions.

Likert Scale Definition

A Likert scale is a type of rating scale that is used to assess opinions, attitudes, or behaviors.

It is made up of a statement or a question, followed by five or seven answer statements. Respondents select the choice that best expresses their feelings about the statement or topic.

Because respondents are given a range of possible responses, Likert scales are excellent for capturing respondents' level of agreement or their thoughts about a topic in a more nuanced manner. Likert scales, on the other hand, are prone to response bias, in which respondents either agree or disagree with all of the items due to weariness or social desirability, or exhibit a proclivity for extreme responses or other demand characteristics.

Likert scales are widely used in survey research, as well as in marketing, psychology, and other social sciences.

When to use Likert Scale?

To comprehend the Likert rating scale, you must first comprehend the concept of a survey scale.

A survey scale is a collection of answer possibilities, either numerical or verbal, that span a wide range of viewpoints on a given issue. It's always part of a closed-ended inquiry (one that gives respondents pre-populated answer options).

So, what precisely is a Likert scale survey question? It's a question with a 5 or 7-point scale, often known as a pleasure scale, that runs from one extreme attitude to the other. Typically, the Likert scale survey question includes a moderate or neutral choice.

Likert scales (named after their originator, American social scientist Rensis Likert) are widely used because they are one of the most dependable methods of measuring attitudes, perceptions, and behaviors.

Likert-type questions, as opposed to binary questions, provide more granular feedback about whether your product was just "good enough" or (hopefully) "excellent." They can also help you decide whether a recent company outing left employees feeling "very satisfied," "somewhat dissatisfied," or perhaps just neutral.

This strategy will allow you to find differences of opinion that could make a significant difference in your understanding of the input you're receiving. It can also show out areas where your service or product could be improved.

Here are the top three Likert Scale Points:

- **Likert Scale of 4 Points**

The four-point Likert scale is essentially a forced Likert scale. It is so named because the user feels compelled to form an opinion. There is no such thing as a safe 'neutral' option. A suitable scale for market researchers, who use the four-point scale to elicit specific reactions.

✓ **Advantages of a 4-point scale**

- The 4-point scale is most appropriate in situations where a specific user opinion is required.
- Best for capturing consumer views on services/products used/experienced.
- Likert scales are often odd-numbered scales. It serves as an exception to the rule.

The disadvantages of a four-point scale

- A four-point Likert scale is found to skew the results.
- When a respondent has no opinion, a four-point Likert scale compels a choice.
- A five-point Likert scale data set is more accurate than a four-point data set.

- Respondents may not respond at all. In many circumstances, knowing that they were impartial is preferable to having them not answer the question at all.

Four-Point Likert Scale Examples

A four-point Likert scale example includes a frequency scale with four options: never, seldom, frequently, and always. A four-point scale example for agreement, with options ranging from strongly disagree to agree, and a four-point Likert scale example for satisfaction, with options ranging from very satisfied to unhappy.

Example of a 4 Point Likert Scale for Frequency

Customer service surveys might utilize an even Likert scale question to measure frequency.

How frequently do you contact customer service?

( ) Never

( ) Rarely

( ) Often

( ) Every time

4 Point Likert Scale Interpretation

• To interpret a four-point scale, assign a point value from 1 to 4 to each response based on the number of responses.

• The most common values for the alternatives are "strongly disagree" at 1 point and "strongly agree" at 4 points.

• Make a table of your results and calculate the Mode (the number of times something happens) and the average response (Mean).

• The mode indicates the most common response to each statement, whereas the mean indicates the overall average response.

5 Point Likert Scale

A five-point Likert scale has five answer alternatives, two extreme poles, a neutral option, and three intermediate answer options. Very satisfied, Satisfied, Neither satisfied nor unsatisfied, unsatisfied, and Very dissatisfied are frequent 5 point Likert scale examples for measuring satisfaction.

Likert's basic 5-point scale has evolved over time. It provides 5 various answer possibilities relating to an agreement for the responders to choose from.

Advantages of a 5-point scale

• It is quite simple for people to grasp.

• For a broader study, a 5-point scale is preferable.

• 5 point Likert scales offer superior data distributions.

The disadvantages of a 5-point Likert scale

• It is occasionally incorrect.

• 5-point scales cannot capture all perspectives on an issue.

• The outcomes of a 5-point scale may not be objective.

Examples of Five Point Likert Scale Questionnaires

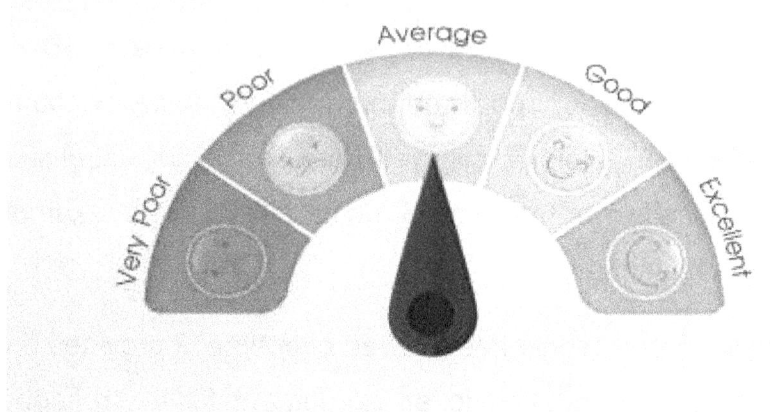

5 Point Likert Scale

Satisfaction	Frequency	Agreement
Very Dissatisfied	Never	Strongly Disagree
Dissatisfied	Rarely	Disagree
Neither Dissatisfied or Satisfied	Sometimes	Neither Disagree or Agree
Satisfied	Often	Agree
Very Satisfied	Always	Strongly Agree

Awareness	Feedback	Likelihood
Not Aware	Not at all helpful	Not Definite
Slightly Aware	Not at all helpful	Not Probable
Moderately aware	Somewhat helpful	Possibly
Aware	Very helpful	Probably
Extremely aware	Extremely helpful	Definitely

Familiarity	Quality	Importance
Not Familiar	Very Poor	Unimportant
Slightly Familiar	Poor	Slightly important
Moderately Familiar	Fair	Moderately important
Familiar	Good	Important
Very Familiar	Excellent	Very Important

How to Interpret a Five-Point Likert Scale Questionnaire

• Based on the number of responses, assign a point value ranging from 1 to 5.

• The alternatives' common values begin with "strongly disagree" at 1 point and end with "strongly agree" at 5.

• Make a table of your results and calculate the Mode (the number of times something happens) and the average response (Mean).

• The mode indicates the most common response to each statement, whereas the mean indicates the overall average response.

Likert Scale (7 Points)

7-point Likert scales are an improvement over 5-point scales. A 7-point Likert scale spans from extreme to extreme, such as "extremely likely" to "not at all likely."

What exactly is a 7-point Likert Scale?

A 7-point Likert scale provides 7 distinct answer alternatives relating to an agreement that are distinct enough for the respondents to avoid confusion. It usually contains a moderate or neutral midpoint, and 7 point Likert scales are the most accurate of the Likert scales.

Rate your level of **mental effort** during this instruction

Hversu mikilli **andlegri áreynslu** varst þú undir á meðan kennslu stóð?

Extremely Low (Mjög Lítilli)	☐ 1	☐ 2	☐ 3	☐ 4	☐ 5	☐ 6	☐ 7	*Extremely High (Mjög Mikilli)*

How **difficult** was this instruction?

Hversu erfitt var kennsluefnið?

Extremely Easy (Mjög auðvelt)	☐ 1	☐ 2	☐ 3	☐ 4	☐ 5	☐ 6	☐ 7	*Extremely Difficult (Mjög erfitt)*

Advantages of a 7-point scale

• It is the most precise Likert scale.

• It is simpler to use.

• It provides a more accurate representation of a respondent's real evaluation.

• The most effective solution for surveys, such as those used in usability testing.

7-point scale's disadvantage

• Previous questions will have an impact on respondents' responses.

Examples of a 7-Point Likert Scale

A 7-point Likert scale example of agreement will include alternatives such as strongly disagree, disagree, slightly disagree, either agree or disagree, somewhat agree, and agree, while 7-point Likert scale examples of frequency and satisfaction will follow the same pattern.

How to Interpret and Analyze a 7-Point Likert Scale

• Based on the number of responses, assign a point value ranging from 1 to 7.

• Assign values to the options, beginning with "strongly disagree" at 1 point and ending with "strongly agree" at 7.

• Make a table of your results and calculate the Mode (the number of times something happens) and the average response (Mean).

• The mode indicates the most common response to each statement, whereas the mean indicates the overall average response.

Other Likert Scale Points are as follows:

- **A two-point Likert scale**

The two-point Likert scale is the most basic type of Likert scale inquiry, with only two Likert alternatives, such as agree and disagree, as the scale's two poles. It is commonly used to assess agreement.

- **Likert Scale of 3 Points**

The three-point Likert scale includes agree and disagree options as well as a neutral option. The 3-point scale, like the 2-point scale, is used to assess agreement. There will be three options: agree, disagree, and neutral.

- **Likert Scale of 6 Points**

A 6-point Likert scale forces decision and produces more accurate results. And, if a neutral is wanted at any moment, the "slightly agree" and "slightly disagree" can be averaged together. Extremely satisfied, Very satisfied, Somewhat satisfied, Somewhat dissatisfied, Very dissatisfied, and Extremely dissatisfied are the options on the 6-point Likert scale.

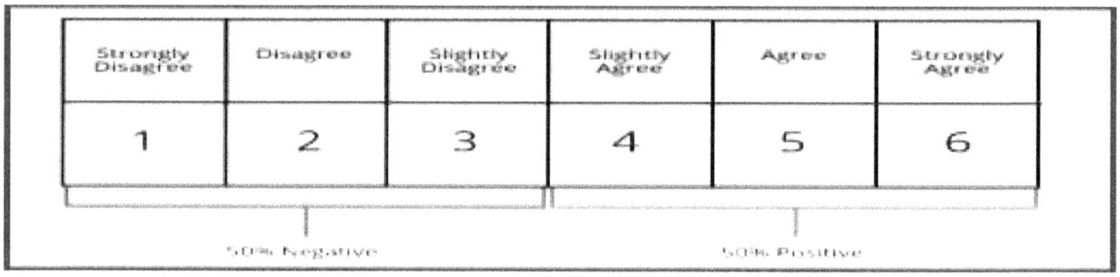

Strongly Disagree	Disagree	Slightly Disagree	Slightly Agree	Agree	Strongly Agree
1	2	3	4	5	6

50% Negative 50% Positive

- **Likert Scale (9 Points)**

The Likert scale has nine points, ranging from 1 (strongly disagree) to 9 (strongly agree). This, in turn, delivers very detailed data and a large range of options to the respondent.

- **Likert Scale (10 Points)**

A 10 point Likert scale has greater variance than a smaller Likert scale, a higher degree of measurement precision, a better chance of detecting changes, and more power to communicate a point of view.

The Advantages of Likert Scales

- ✓ ***Likert scale ratings are designed to provide quantitative answer possibilities that facilitate data analysis. Respondents also have a variety of responses that are more particular to their feelings about a product or service.***

One advantage of using the Likert scale is that it can help you avoid some of the classic problems of survey design, such as asking overly broad questions that respondents may find difficult to answer. This may cause users to become frustrated and respond too soon, compromising the quality of your data.

Survey designers in a hurry may resort to larger sorts of questions, such as "yes/no," "select all," open-ended, ranking, or matrix questions, as a sort of survey shortcut.

As a general rule, they should count on their old his companion the Likert scale, which will keep the responder focused and delighted with its straightforward, clear language.

- ✓ ***Likert scale inquiries keep your respondents satisfied while also improving data quality.***

  It is critical that each series of questions in your survey be focused on the same topic. Finally, this will assist you obtain more accurate results. Why? Because when it comes time to report the data, you'll want to look at a score that combines the answers to a few questions.

- ✓ ***When inquiries are focused on a single topic, Likert scales function well.***

  When you group questions about one topic together and total all their replies to produce a score--in this case, a "Quality of Food" score--you'll gain a more reliable gauge of attitudes toward the specific product, service, or event you're researching.

- ✓ ***Use cases and illustrations of the Likert scale***

  Likert scale questions are utilized in a variety of surveys, whether you want to know how your employees feel about their jobs or what your customers think about your latest product.

How to Create Likert Scale Questionnaires

- **Determine the purpose of the Likert Scale.**
  What do you wish to learn? Assume you've seen that some people enjoy online shopping while others would not do it if their life depended on it. You also want to quantify this.

- **Make a list of indicator statements.**
  Remember that a Likert scale survey is best used when you want to learn about something that cannot be explained with a single question. That means you'll need to collect indicators—specific types of inquiries that will assist you comprehend the notion you're attempting to quantify.
  - Consider client satisfaction. Likert scale questions are ideal for conducting a customer satisfaction survey since numerous factors might influence the phenomenon, such perceived quality, customer expectations, cost, timeliness of service or delivery, and so on. Each of these is an indicator of customer satisfaction—you can learn if the consumer is generally pleased with their purchase or is extremely disappointed.
  - So, what kind of questions can you ask people to find out how much they enjoy shopping online?
  - Begin by asking them to list terms that they connect with internet shopping, such as dull, complicated, easy, quick, intangible, and so on—you want to evaluate the respondent's view here.
  - Create the indicator statements, often known as Likert items, around this list.
    1. I prefer touching items before purchasing them (Strongly Agree—Strongly Disagree)

2. The number of possibilities available on the internet overwhelms me (Strongly Agree—Strongly Disagree)
3. Checking out online is simple (Strongly Agree—Strongly Disagree)
   - It is critical that each sentence gets to the essence of what you want to learn.

Here are some more pointers for writing indicator statements:

- For balance, use both positive and negative signs. A positively phrased remark should be followed with a negatively phrased statement later in the inquiry.

So, if you have the statement, "The variety of options online overwhelms me," you should also have the item, "I appreciate the wide selection online shopping has to offer."

Positive remarks should be agreed upon by those who disagree with negative assertions, and vice versa. That is how you may be certain that your queries are clear and the solutions are trustworthy.

- When writing survey questions, adhere to best practices. Consider your audience's language and avoid double-barreled or long, convoluted phrases.

Remember that the way we phrase a question affects the response. So use neutral language and avoid words such as 'love,' 'hate,' 'awful,' 'amazing,' and so on. Instead of cueing it in the sentences, let them tell you how strong their feelings are.

- **Choose the appropriate response scale.**

When it comes to Likert-type response ordinal scales, there are two options.

The first is a semantic scale. You want alternatives that are straightforward and unambiguous. Among the most prevalent are the following: Agree—Disagree, Helpful—Not Helpful, Excellent—Poor, Satisfied—Dissatisfied, and Always—Never. However, just because they are popular does not imply that they are correct.

Also, ensure that the distinctions between the categories are valid and relevant. Assume you want to know how frequently a person gets up from their desk at work. You select Never—Seldom—Sometimes—Frequently—Always. How can you measure the difference between rarely and occasionally?

If a scale's connotations are unclear, either explain them in your introduction or modify the scale. Don't say 'Sometimes' when you mean 'Once a week.'

The second factor is the amount of response options. Likert-type responses frequently feature an odd number, giving responders a neutral alternative. The jury is still out on whether or not this is required or even desirable.

Most academics agree that a 5-point Likert scale survey is the bare minimum. However, other study indicates that the more options there are, the less frequently respondents choose the middle or neutral category. What is certain is that a 7-point Likert scale approaches the upper limits of reliability—so adding additional options is likely to result in worse, rather than better, Likert scale results.

- **Trial test, and test again**

  Surveys are a continuous process. The key to conducting good research is to test, analyze, revise, and improve your data collection methods.

  Test your survey on a small sample of people who represent the larger group you're attempting to learn more about, and then analyze the results. If you want to earn extra credit, you can perform an item analysis.

  An item analysis can assist you in determining which items, or claims, are the most valuable and which are troublesome. The math is difficult (which is why I left psychology), but a statistical analysis tool can assist you in determining the correlations between your queries.

  Once the survey has begun, run another item analysis to confirm that the scale is consistent.

- **Be precise.**

To avoid confusion and maximize their usefulness, Likert-type questions must be phrased correctly. When you inquire about restaurant service satisfaction, do you mean service from valets, servers, or the host? Is it all of the above? Are you wondering if the consumer was pleased with the timeliness of service, the courtesy of the attendants, or the quality of the food and beverages? Bottom line: If you can be more specific, your Likert questions will likely yield more valuable responses.

- **Be cautious while using adjectives**.

When using language to ask about concepts in your survey, make certain that respondents understand exactly what you mean. Your response options must include descriptive terms that are simple to understand. There should be no doubt as to which grade is higher or larger than the next: Is "pretty much" greater than "quite a bit"? It's best to start with the extremes ("extremely," "not at all"), then set the midpoint of your scale to indicate moderation ("moderately," "neither agree nor disagree,") and then use very unambiguous terms-"very," "slightly"-for the remaining possibilities.

- **It is preferable to inquire.**

Because humans are typically pleasant and respectful, statements carry an inherent risk: most people will tend to agree with them rather than argue with them. (This is known as acquiescence response bias.) It is therefore more effective to ask a question rather than make a statement.

- **Additional hints for using Likert scales**
- ***Maintain the labeling***. Numbered scales that solely utilize numbers as response options rather than words may cause confusion among survey respondents since they may not know which end of the range is positive or negative.
- ***Keep it distinctive***. Scales with an odd number of values will have a midpoint. How many options should you provide people? Respondents have difficulties defining their perspective of view on a scale greater than seven. If you give people more than seven response options, they are more likely to pick an answer at random, rendering your data worthless. Our methodologists advocate five scale points for a unipolar scale and seven scale points for a bipolar scale.
- ***Keep it continuous***. Response options on a scale should be similarly spaced from one another. When utilizing word labels instead of numbers, this can be difficult, so make sure you understand what your words imply.

- ***Maintain inclusivity.*** Scales should cover the complete range of possible responses. If a question asks how quick your waiter was and the responses range from "extremely quick" to "moderately quick," respondents who believe the waiter was slow will be unsure which option to select.
- ***Maintain rationality.*** Add skip logic to save your survey respondents time. For example, suppose you want to know how much your customer enjoyed your restaurant, but you only want extra information if they were dissatisfied with something. Use question logic to ensure that only individuals who are dissatisfied skip to a question asking for suggestions for improvement.

Exercise 5

1. Discuss the primary benefits of using Likert scale?	2. What are the limitations of Likert scale?

3. Briefly discuss the process involve in creating Likert scale questionnaires.	4. Explain the different characteristics of a good Likert scale questionnaires.
5. What are the factors to consider while utilizing a Likert scale?	**6. Why is a trial test necessary after drafting Likert scale questions?**

7. Explain the various indicators to be considered while creating Likert scale statements.	**8. Give some pointers for designing Likert scale questions.**

CHAPTER 6

Demographic Survey questions

Introduction:

In our ever-evolving society, it is crucial for individuals, organizations, and institutions alike to comprehend the intricacies of our demographic landscape. Unveiling the various facets of our diverse population not only grants us an enhanced understanding of the world we inhabit, but it also facilitates the creation of inclusive environments, policies, and strategies that cater to the needs, aspirations, and challenges of different groups.

Chapter 6 delves deep into the realm of demographic survey questions, illuminating their significance as powerful tools for uncovering invaluable insights and charting the course of progress. Through a comprehensive exploration of the intricacies of collecting demographic data, we will unveil the immense importance of understanding the multifaceted identities and experiences that shape our communities.

The chapter begins by elucidating the fundamental objectives behind conducting demographic surveys and why they are essential for policymakers, researchers, and industries across a wide range of sectors. We will explore how these surveys enable us to paint an accurate, vivid portrait of our society by examining key demographic variables such as age, gender, ethnicity, education, income, and more.

By understanding the significance of accurate demographic data, we can shed light on systemic disparities, identify areas of improvement, and foster a society that champions inclusivity and equal opportunities for all. Whether you are a researcher aiming to gather rich and representative data or a decision-maker striving to create policies that empower every individual, this chapter equips you with the necessary tools to navigate the intricate world of demographic survey questions.

So, let us embark on this enlightening journey together, as we unravel the power, potential, and pitfalls of understanding our demographic landscape through surveys. With each word, let us draw closer to a society that celebrates its diversity and works tirelessly towards a fairer, more harmonious future for all.

What are demographic survey questions?

Demographics are the characteristics of a population that have been classified according to specific criteria, such as age, gender, and income, in order to research the features of a specific group. Demographic data analysis is critical for corporations, organizations, and governments to make decisions. Businesses can use this data to develop marketing strategies, while governments can use it to promote public policy.

Demographic survey questions are used to elicit more personal information from survey participants. The majority of demographic inquiries inquire about age, gender, occupation, income, education level, and ethnicity.

However, being confined to boxes and endless spreadsheets is not a pleasant experience. As a result, it's not surprising that people frequently abandon demographic questionnaires. Often, it comes directly after the first question, which asks for something personal, such as their annual income—which, in certain countries, is considered as impolite as criticizing their mother.

So, how can you design demographic questions that everyone can answer? You don't want someone to think, "How dare they ask me that?"

We define demographics, explain why they are essential, and demonstrate how they are utilized to understand and help the general people.

- **Demographics** refer to the precise features of a given population and include factors like age, income level, and geographic region.
- Focus groups, surveys and polls, census collection, and psychographic research are all methods for gathering **demographic** data.
- **Demographic** data can be utilized to develop effective marketing efforts, economic analyses, and government policies.

What are Demographics?

Demographics refer to a population's numerous traits. Factors such as the race, gender, and age of a group being examined are examples of demographics. Demographic data is statistical information about the socioeconomic status of the population.

Demographic data can contain particular information about a population's characteristics, such as the following examples:

- Age group
- Race and ethnic origin
- Gender

- Education level
- Income
- Employment situation
- Occupation
- Homeownership
- Birth order
- Civil Status

Methods for gathering demographic information

There are various typical methods for gathering demographic information. The following are the most prevalent methods:

- **Surveys:**

Organizations may conduct consumer surveys or assessments to collect information about what individuals buy, why they have certain buying habits, and how much money they spend on average. A company can also get demographic information by monitoring its social media accounts and e-commerce website. As consumers become more comfortable sharing a variety of personal information online, online forms and email marketing can be used to obtain more accurate and valuable data.

Census:

Direct demographic data collection include recording and researching official records of births, marriages, divorces, deaths, and migrations. The United States Census Bureau counts the population of the United States by conducting a census every ten years, in addition to collecting annual statistical data and conducting regular surveys.

Online polls:

Online demographic data gathering is becoming more popular, because to the ease and low cost of running online surveys. Due to the limits of this single-such as mixed-mode surveys, can be coupled for improved representation.

Group discussions:

Organizing focus groups to discuss a specific product or service is an efficient approach of gathering demographic data. Focus groups can be used to examine how people in specific demographic groups respond to a product or service, and this method is invaluable in gathering critical input from participants that can aid a firm before launching their product or service.

What is the primary function of demographic information (age, gender, marital status, etc.) **in a research study?**

When should demographic questions be included?

- ✓ Demographic variables are frequently used as part of the analyses - usually as potentially influential independent variables." In this case, they are often referred to as "control variables" or "background variables," so that their influence is removed (i.e., controlled for) before assessing the effects of your substantive independent variables.
- ✓ One of the primary reasons for gathering such data is to be able to describe the kind of persons that took part in the study. Consider not knowing if they were all guys or all girls. Or not knowing their ages, including the age distribution in a sample. Or not knowing if two groups being compared had backgrounds that were sufficiently similar or not. And so forth.
- ✓ Aside from that, demographic variables are frequently employed in analyses, usually as potentially influential independent variables.
- ✓ The collection and analysis of demographic data gives information on migration and movement shifts and patterns. This

would aid municipal planners in resource allocation for social services, business, public health, education, and so on.

- ✓ Demographic data can be used to plan future studies and could be used in a stratified sample strategy (if applicable).
- ✓ Demographic factors are frequently employed in analyses, usually as potentially influential independent variables.
- ✓ The description or distribution of characteristics of a desired demographic, customer base, or population is referred to as demographics. Socioeconomic data is used by governments to better understand the age, racial makeup, and income distribution (among other variables) in communities, cities, states, and nations in order to make better public policy decisions.
- ✓ Demographics are used by organizations to create more successful marketing and advertising campaigns and to analyze patterns among various target groups.

Exercise 6:

1. Discuss the uses of demographics in research.	2. Why is demographics important in research?
3. Describe the primary information contained in demographics.	4. Differentiate between survey and census methods.

5. How are online survey polls carried out?	**6. Explain the advantages and disadvantages of group discussions.**
7.When are demographic inquiries appropriate?	**8. Explain how demographic data is used in research.**

CHAPTER 7

Data Collection Issues

Introduction:

In this chapter, we delve into the essential topic of issues on data collection in statistics. We explore the intricacies involved in ensuring accurate and reliable data, as well as the potential pitfalls that researchers and statisticians may encounter. By understanding these issues, professionals in the field can navigate the data collection process more effectively and reduce the likelihood of biased or flawed results.

One of the central issues addressed in this chapter is the problem of obtaining representative samples. When collecting data, it is crucial to ensure that the sample chosen is representative of the population under study. Failure to do so may lead to biased or ungeneralizable results, limiting the usefulness of statistical analyses. We will explore techniques and considerations for achieving a representative sample, such as random sampling, stratified sampling, and sample size determination.

Another significant concern in data collection is ensuring the quality and reliability of the collected data. Factors such as incomplete responses, respondent bias, measurement errors, and selection bias can introduce inaccuracies and affect the credibility of statistical analyses. We will discuss methods to minimize these errors, including careful questionnaire design, meticulous data entry, and thorough validation procedures.

Moreover, this chapter delves into the ethical considerations surrounding data collection. In an era of increasing privacy concerns, researchers must navigate the fine line between obtaining valuable data and respecting the rights and privacy of individuals involved. We will explore strategies for obtaining informed consent, protecting data confidentiality, and ensuring ethical practices throughout the data collection process.

Finally, this chapter also addresses the issue of data collection in various research settings, including surveys, experiments, observational studies, and secondary data analysis. Each approach presents unique challenges and considerations that statisticians must be aware of to ensure accurate and reliable findings. By exploring these different scenarios, readers will gain a comprehensive understanding of the challenges and best practices of data collection in different contexts.

Through a thorough examination of the issues on data collection in statistics, this chapter aims to equip researchers, statisticians, and analysts with the knowledge and tools necessary to improve the quality and credibility of their research. By addressing representative sampling, data quality control, ethical considerations, and research settings, we lay the foundation for effective data collection practices and set the stage for meaningful and reliable statistical analyses.

In order to plan for the data collection phase of the research, there are several issues which need to be addressed. These include the following:

- ***What data do we gather?***

  This topic has been discussed in detail in previous chapters. It entails converting concepts into operational indications. It also entails identifying and defining variables to be collected in the study.

➢ *How do we collect the data?*

The "how" question has two components: the mode of data collection and the study design.
There are three primary methods for gathering data: checking records, asking people questions, and witnessing or capturing events as they occur. Because the data already exists and only has to be retrieved, conducting a records review is the cheapest and quickest approach to acquire it. However, major issues with this kind of data gathering include record incompleteness, non-comparability of definitions, and difficulties validating information.
There are several methods for asking individuals questions, including personal interviews, self-administered questionnaires, and group discussions such as focus and nominal groups, which are qualitative modalities of data collecting.

Observing and/or documenting events as they occur is a common practice in qualitative research, particularly ethnography. It can give a more detailed view of non-quantitative phenomena. However, strict training of data collectors is required, especially since assuring objectivity of observations may be a challenge.
There are several methods for asking individuals questions, including personal interviews, self-administered questionnaires, and group discussions such as focus and nominal groups, which are qualitative modalities of data collecting.

The following are some design concerns that could arise:
• Using primary versus secondary data
• Experimental vs. observational
• Cross-sectional versus longitudinal data
• Paired/Related Samples vs. Independent Samples

- Including or excluding a control group
- Quantitative vs. qualitative methods

The data collector distinguishes between main and secondary data. Primary data are new data gathered by the Research Team throughout the course of the study, and secondary data are previously collected data by others. In the case of related and independent samples, these are characteristics of samples representing various groups included in the study, regardless of whether they are linked or independent of one another. For example, in a study to establish whether a person's position influences his blood pressure level, the researcher has two methods for selecting samples for his study. He can gather three different groups of people and have them stand in three different positions while their blood pressures are taken - one group lying down, one group sitting down, and one group standing up. Independent samples are obtained when the samples for each group are chosen independently of one another. The issue that occasionally arises with independent samples is non-comparability between them in terms of a variable that impacts the study's outcomes. In our example, if the three groups are not equivalent in terms of age, any differences in blood pressure levels seen between them may be attributed to their age rather than differences in their position. To circumvent this issue, the researcher can use related samples instead. Instead of three groups of samples, he can use just one and assess the blood pressure of the same person in three distinct positions. Because the three blood pressure readings belong to the same person, the issue of comparability is avoided. .In this example, another option to have similar samples is to employ three groups of people in three distinct positions, but match the groups based on sex and age, which are characteristics closely associated to blood pressure.

- ***Who do we collect data from?***

This problem concerns the selection of the best suited respondent. This is especially important when the subjects of the study are unable to provide answers (e.g., babies, sick elderly).

- ***Who should be in charge of gathering data?***

When deciding who should collect data, important issues to consider are required skills, cost, and potential biases. Because of their knowledge with the area and the population, it is customary to engage existing service providers and field workers in a community, such as midwives or BHWs, as interviewers for a survey. However, if the purpose of the survey is to assess the quality of health care received by the community, using service providers to conduct household interviews may bring bias into the study.

- ***When and how frequently should data be gathered?***

The frequency and timing of data collection are determined by the study's objectives, study design, and variable(s) being gathered. In general, data collection timeliness is not a major concern, unless the variable being researched is modified by time or seasonal patterns.

- ***Where should information be gathered?***

The decision of whether to conduct the interview at the subject's house, the health facility, or a public meeting venue (for example, Barangay Hall) involves logistical considerations, as well as the requirement to optimize study yield while minimizing biases. An important issue to consider is whether data collection can be implemented so that the target population (population to which study results will be generalized) will be the same as the sampling population (population from which the samples are taken.

- ***What procedures, actions, or methods are required to reduce data gathering issues?***

Memory/recall bias, lack of collaboration, the Hawthorne effect, and observer prejudice are all common challenges and biases encountered during data gathering. The Hawthorne effect describes how people change their behavior when they are observed. Designing techniques to reduce these biases is part of the data collecting planning process.

Guidelines for developing and structuring questions

General principles:

- Keep in mind that the goal of building data collecting tools is to get complete and accurate information that is relevant to the data collection activity's objectives.
- Keep in mind that by supplying the relevant information, the respondent is assisting the data collector.
- Explain the reason each question or item in the data collection tool is important.
- Avoid queries that are unnecessary or irrelevant.
- To the greatest extent feasible, avoid "back-rider" queries. These are questions that were added at the request of friends or because there is an opportunity to ask them. The majority of back-rider questions turn out to be irrelevant to the survey's original purpose.
- Be aware of any privacy issues the respondent may have. Respect the respondent's freedom to refuse to answer inquiries that they believe are an invasion of their privacy.
- Empathy - when building the data collection instrument, consider yourself as a respondent. Consider if you would answer this question if you were the respondent.

Question structure

- When selecting the order of the questions or items in the data collecting instrument, begin with those that are simple to administer or answer. The first questions should aim to pique the respondent's interest and motivation, as well as to instill confidence in the data collection activity.
- A sequence of lead-in questions should ease respondents into awkward or sensitive questions. Do not knock on someone's door and then ask, "Have you ever had an abortion?"
- Items or questions should be arranged according to subject areas to avoid an unnatural flow. Do not jump from one topic to another.
- A good data collection tool should be simple to use. Examples of how to accomplish this include:
  - ✓ Important words and phrases should be underlined or printed in italics, and instructions to interviewers should be written entirely in capital letters.
- An excellent data collection tool is also simple to use. This is accomplished by using the:
  - ✓ Application of instructions
  - ✓ Numbering in a sequential order
  - ✓ Indentation
- Keep the principles of data processing in mind when creating the format and list of response possibilities for closed-ended questions.

Question Phrases

- Avoid questions that are confusing due to an insufficient frame of reference (for example, "How frequently were you sick?").
- Avoid "multi-barreled" questions. These are inquiries that request multiple items at the same time. "How many times do

you eat meat, fish, vegetables, fruits, eggs, and cheese?" is an example of this type of question.

- Avoid asking "leading" questions. These are questions that are phrased in such a way that the respondent understands the expected response and is encouraged to offer it.
- Be cautious with questions that require responders to recollect events or facts that occurred in the past. This is the most likely time for you to incur recall or memory bias. By associating dates with key occurrences, the respondent can be assisted in recalling events.
- Use simple, common words that responders may use in a conversation. Technical jargon, formal language, and colloquialism should be avoided. In a breastfeeding survey, for example, do not use the phrase "colostrum" to refer to the mother's first milk because very few moms would grasp the technical term.

Creating pre-defined categories for survey responses

- When asking questions that require responders to choose from a pre-defined set of solutions, ensure that the categories are exhaustive and mutually exclusive. Exhaustive indicates that the pre-set categories must account for all conceivable answers, so that each response has a corresponding category. Mutually exclusive means that there is no overlap of categories, so each response can be classified in just one category.
- When asking respondents to answer to statements using a Likert scale, ensure that both the statement to which the respondent is asked to react and the options offered in the form of a Likert scale are adequate for this type of measurement.

Exercise 7

1. Give 5 Examples of Double Barreled Questions.	2. Discuss the importance of wording in question construction.
3. Discuss the issue on where should the data collection be conducted?	4. What is the importance of question phrasing in data collection?

5. **Give three examples of pre-defined category response in question formulation.**	6. **Discuss the different guidelines in developing and phrasing questions for data collection.**

REFERENCES

Aday, L.A. (1996). *Designing and Conducting Health Surveys A Comprehensive Guide (Second Edition).* Jossey-Bass Publishers. San Francisco.

Warwick, D. and Lininger, C. (1975). *The Sample Survey: Theory and Practice.* McGraw Hill Book Company. New York.

Bowling, A. (1997). *Research Methods in Health*. Buckingham: Open University Press.

Burns, N., & Grove, S. K. (1997). *The Practice of Nursing Research Conduct, Critique, & Utilization*. Philadelphia: W.B. Saunders and Co.

Jamieson, S. (2004). Likert scales: how to (ab) use them. *Medical Education, 38(12)*, 1217-1218.

Likert, R. (1932). A Technique for the Measurement of Attitudes. *Archives of Psychology*, 140, 1–55.

About the Authors

Hilaria M. Barsabal, a highly accomplished author and esteemed academician. With a wealth of knowledge and experience, she has made significant contributions to the field of education and mathematics.

She holds an impressive educational background, starting with her Bachelor of Science degree in Mathematics. Further expanding her expertise, she pursued a Master of Arts in Education majoring in Mathematics, followed by a Master of Business Administration. Currently, she is finalizing her dissertation for the Doctor of Philosophy in Education majoring in Educational Management, demonstrating her commitment to continuous learning and research.

She has held a number of important positions in academia during the course of her 34-year career. Notably, she is currently serving as Cagayan State University's University Director for Quality Assurance. In her job, she is responsible for the upkeep and improvement of academic standards, ensuring that pupils receive a high-quality education.

She has taught subjects such as Biostatistics, Financial Management, Investment Management, and Business Statistics at both the undergraduate and graduate levels during her career. Her dedication to influencing the brains of future professionals and her significant teaching expertise demonstrate her enthusiasm for education.

She is a prolific author in addition to her esteemed position and academic accomplishments. Her books and research papers have made significant contributions to the domains of mathematics, education, and educational management. She contributes unique ideas and ways to the academic community by drawing on her considerable experience.

She is a respected person in the field due to her excellent mathematical basis and profound understanding of educational and managerial ideas. She motivates students, academics, and educators alike through her work, leaving an indelible impression on the academic world.

Mariden V. Cauilan is a well-known novelist with a strong academic background. She has a Bachelor's degree in Mathematics as well as Master's and Doctoral degrees in Public Administration, giving her a diversified skill set that spans numerous disciplines.

She has displayed remarkable leadership and innovation in altering the educational environment as the Vice President for Academic Affairs at Cagayan State University. She also works as a faculty member at the university's graduate level, passing on knowledge and sharpening students' academic abilities.

With over three decades of experience as a thesis and dissertation adviser, she has helped numerous scholars achieve their research goals. Her guidance and expertise have been instrumental in producing high-quality academic works. Recognized as a seasoned research consultant, she is regarded as a trusted source of invaluable insights.

She has made an unforgettable imprint on the academic community throughout their prolific career. She is a prominent author whose contributions to the fields of Mathematics and Public Administration have substantially advanced.

www.ingramcontent.com/pod-product-compliance
Lightning Source LLC
LaVergne TN
LVHW080554160826
845677LV00010B/1844

9786214708147